Nature's Children

KOALAS

Elizabeth MacLeod

 Grolier

FACTS IN BRIEF

Classification of the Koala

    Class: *Mammalia* (mammals)
    Order: *Marsupialia* (pouch-bearing mammals)
    Family: *Phascolarctidae* (koala family)
    Genus: *Phascolarctos*
    Species: *Phascolarctos cinerus*

World distribution.   Australia.

Habitat.   Eucalyptus forests.

Distinctive physical characteristics.   Koalas have reddish or gray coats that are lighter on the ears and underside, long strong claws and cheek pouches in which they can store food. The females have pouches on their stomachs in which they carry their young during the first part of their lives.

Habits.   Koalas are solitary creatures who spend most of their time eating, sleeping, or looking for food. They are most active at night, feeding and defending their territories.

Diet.   The leaves of the eucalyptus tree.

Published originally as
"Getting to Know . . . Nature's Children."

This series is approved and recommended by the Federation of Ontario Naturalists.

This library reinforced edition is available exclusively from:

 Grolier Educational Corporation
Sherman Turnpike, Danbury, Connecticut 06816

Contents

11/94 Grolier (direct) 89.95

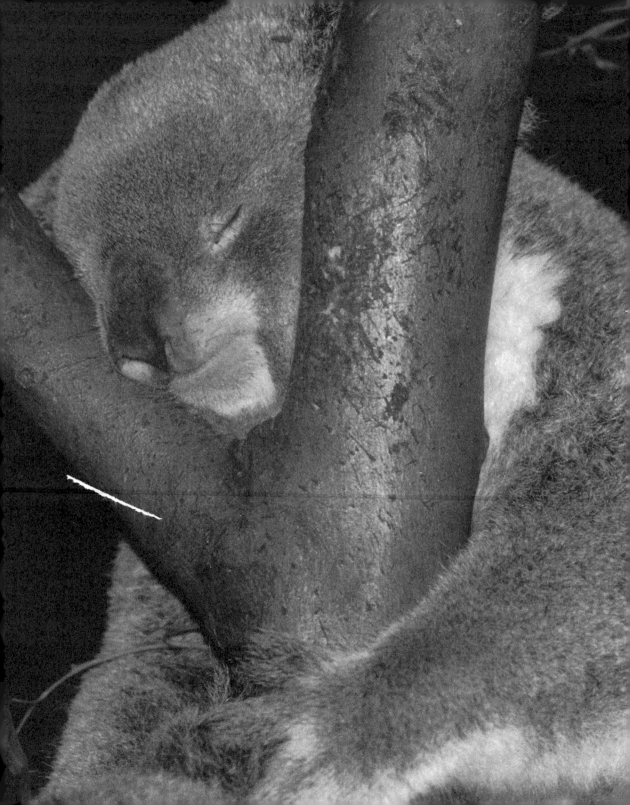

High up in a tall tree, a fluffy gray ball sits wedged in a fork of the branches. Slowly the ball begins to uncurl and soon you can see a sleepy-looking face and four furry legs. It's a koala waking up and it's already reaching for a branch of eucalyptus leaves to munch.

Koala is an Australian aboriginal word that means "animal that does not drink." It's true that koalas rarely drink—they get all the water they need from the juicy eucalyptus leaves they eat. And eating eucalyptus leaves is one of a koala's favorite things to do.

If you would like to find out more about koalas and how they live, just turn the page.

Cuddly Cubs

A young koala usually rides on its mom's back as she moves around the treetops in search of food. Clinging to her fur, the little one feels safe and protected. It will be several months before the cub is brave enough to let go and start exploring the world by itself.

If the cub should get lost or need help, it will cry until its mother comes to the rescue. People who have heard a young koala's distress call say it sounds almost exactly like the cry of a human baby!

Hitching a ride!

Animals with Pouches

Many people call koalas "koala bears" but they aren't bears at all. Koalas belong to a group of animals called marsupials. These animals give birth to young that are so tiny the mother has to shelter them in a pouch for several months while they finish developing. Kangaroos, wallabies and opossums are other marsupials.

Most scientists think that the koala's closest relative is the wombat, a stout, large-nosed animal that lives on the ground. Even though koalas live in trees, they have many things in common with wombats, including downward-facing pouches. You might think that the koala baby would fall out of a pouch that opens downward, but the cub is safe and snug inside. Later you'll see why this is the perfect pocket for a koala.

The shy wombat leaves its underground burrow at night to feed on grass, bark and roots.

Home Down Under

Australia is the only place to find koalas in the wild. They once lived in many places on that island continent, but now they can only be found along its east coast. The koalas that live to the north where the climate is warm have reddish fur coats that are short and light. Southern koalas have dark gray fur and are larger than their northern cousins. And since these southern koalas face colder weather, their fur is longer and thicker.

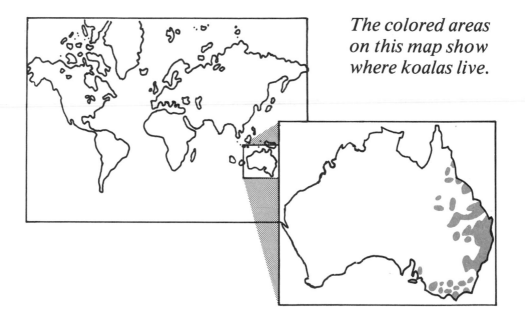

The colored areas on this map show where koalas live.

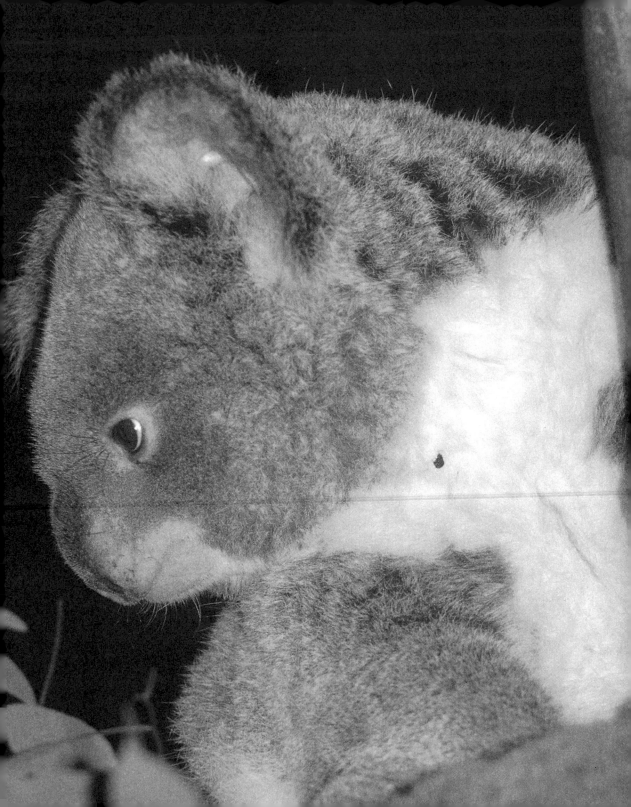

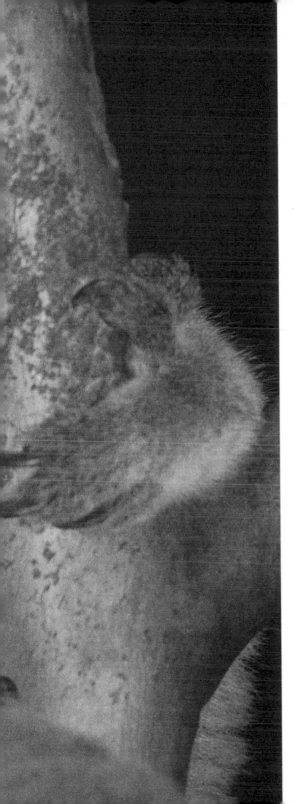

Treetop Territory

Although a koala does have a territory it calls home, it does not make a den or nest and it doesn't even claim a particular tree as its own. But koalas are not very sociable. A male koala may share a territory with two or three females as well as some younger males, but they all do their best to avoid one another. In fact, two koalas rarely sleep or even feed in the same tree unless it is very big. The koala that is already in the tree will growl a warning to any new arrival to "Keep moving!"

Some koalas may stick together, but usually they ignore each other unless it's mating season.

Koalas Up Close

Most people find koalas very appealing. Their sleepy, blinking eyes make them look wise, and their fluffy fur makes you want to pick them up and cuddle them.

An adult koala is about the size of a large bulldog. A male may weigh up to 14 kilograms (30 pounds), about as much as an average three-year-old child. Females are smaller and weigh less than males.

The fur on a koala's stomach and the long fur on its ears tend to be a lighter color than the rest of its fur. There are also usually white patches on its rump. This dappled fur probably helps camouflage the koala. An animal looking up from below would find it hard to see the koala against the shadows of the leaves. A koala has only a short, stumpy tail so there is nothing to get in the way when it sits in a tree.

Koalas have very strong arm and shoulder muscles, ideal for climbing and hanging on to trees.

Super Sniffer

Koalas are born with a good sense of smell, and they never lose it. Adults can easily sniff out the nearest food tree or tell how many koalas are nearby. They also have a keen sense of hearing because their large ears help focus sound.

Koalas are most active at night, especially just after sunset. Like most nocturnal animals, they don't rely very much on their eyesight. In fact, compared to other creatures of the night, their eyes are very small.

A nose for what's happening.

Front paw

Back paw

Handy Paws

A koala has multi-purpose paws. The fingers of its front paws are separated into two groups, with the first two fingers divided from the other three. This makes these paws especially good for grasping and climbing.

On the koala's back feet, the first toe sticks out in much the same way as your thumb. Like you, the koala uses its "thumb" to hold on to things. It uses its second and third toes, which are joined together, to comb its fur. The fourth and fifth toes have strong claws and are good for climbing.

Both the front and back paws have thick rough pads on the bottom. These help the koala grip branches and tree trunks as it moves about. They also act as cushions when it leaps from branch to branch. As well, the koala's long, strong claws not only help it to hold on when climbing, but also help it defend itself against enemies such as wild dogs, large birds and giant lizards.

Mother koala must hold on tight with the extra weight on her back.

Getting Around in the Trees

With its incredible sense of balance, a koala is completely at home eating, sleeping and moving about high in the trees. When it wants to move to a new tree, the koala climbs along a branch until it bends and touches the branches of the next tree. Then the koala climbs along this "bridge" into the new tree and promptly starts munching.

A koala is a speedy climber. Clasping the tree trunk with its front claws, it quickly pulls up its hind legs to its front paws. All this happens so fast, it looks as if the koala is leaping up the tree.

Getting Around Below

When a koala runs out of nearby trees to climb, it must come down to the ground. Slowly and carefully it backs down the tree. Once it hits the ground, it quickly bounds over to the nearest feeding tree and leaps to safety.

Believe it or not, a koala is also a strong swimmer. It looks very clumsy as it slowly paddles through the water, with just a little of its head showing. Once it reaches land, it shakes itself so hard to dry off that its ears slap against its head!

Heading for cover!

Look Out!

If you ever visit Australia, keep your eyes open
for this sign by the roadside. Koalas don't like
moving through thick bushes and grasses so
they'll often walk on roads. They don't seem to
be at all disturbed by cars and will even cause
traffic jams by sitting down in the middle of the
road! Usually no one wants to try to move a
koala since it can put up quite a fight with its
strong, sharp claws. Instead, traffic waits until
the koala has finished resting.

*Koalas may live up to 20 years in
the wild.*

Leafy Lunch

A koala eats almost nothing but the leaves of eucalyptus trees. And not just any eucalyptus tree. This little animal is a very picky eater and will munch on only certain leaves of certain trees.

Although most other animals find eucalyptus leaves bad tasting and can't digest them, a koala has a special stomach that lets it eat these leaves. But it must be careful. Why? The younger leaves contain a deadly poison. Koalas quickly learn to eat only the older leaves that have lost most of the poison.

Powerful jaw muscles and strong biting and grinding teeth help the koala eat up to one kilogram (2 pounds) of eucalyptus leaves each day. This furry muncher uses pouches in its cheeks to store food as it chews.

There is not much nutritional value in eucalyptus leaves, that's why koalas must eat so many.

Coughdrop Coat

The oily eucalyptus leaves provide koalas with more than just the food and water they need. The strong-smelling oils in the leaves give koalas their characteristic coughdrop smell. It's a very strong odor and can be rather unpleasant, but it keeps fleas and parasites out of the koala's beautiful, soft fur.

Is there anything cuter?

Z-z-z-z-z-z

Koalas sleep up to 18 hours each day, usually waking up only to eat. What a life!

Most koalas like to sleep high in the trees, and they usually don't bother to try and hide from enemies. They just nestle into the fork of a tree or wrap themselves around a branch with their paws folded together or hanging down loosely. Or a koala may sleep resting on the pad of thickened skin at the base of its back. It may lean its head against a branch to be more secure, but doesn't always.

In fact, koalas can fall asleep in almost any position. Sometimes they even fall asleep in the middle of eating! You can see leaves hanging out of their mouths as they doze. Or a baby may fall asleep with its little head hanging out of its mother's pouch.

Falling asleep on the job.

Beat the Heat

Summer in Australia can be extremely hot, and the koala can find its thick fur coat very uncomfortable. If the day really warms up, a koala may move from the eucalyptus tree where it spent the night feeding to a leafier tree that provides more shade. There it sprawls along the branch in a position that will shade it from the sun. When it is really hot, the koala eats much less and only moves to find a cooler spot.

Noisy Neighbors

Koalas are quiet most of the day, but when night falls they can be very noisy. Males are especially loud and will warn other males away from their trees with harsh grating noises that sound like a handsaw going through wood. During the mating season, a male tries to attract females to him by using low roars, bellows and mews. He may also use a cry that sounds a bit like a sneeze and another that sounds like loud ticking. A female will roar and croon in response until the two find each other.

Sounding off.

Summer Romance

Mating season for koalas is spring and summer, which in Australia is September to February. Each male patrols his territory carefully, looking for females. To mark the boundaries of his territory, the male rubs a gland on his chest against the trees. This scent marker warns other males to keep away. Fights often break out between the males at this time and can be quite vicious.

Koalas only stay together to mate. When the baby is born a little over a month later, the female raises it on her own.

Treetop mates.

Incredible Journey

Mother koalas usually give birth to only one cub every other year. Before the baby is born, mom carefully cleans out her pouch. The pouch is tough and elastic. Once it is thoroughly clean, the mother koala licks a trail to her pouch for her baby to follow.

When the baby is born, it is about the size and shape of a small jellybean. It is pink, hairless and glistening wet. The baby's back legs are just bumps, but its front paws and arms are well developed. It will need them to help pull itself to its mother's pouch. The baby almost looks like it is swimming through the fur on its mother's belly.

Although the tiny traveler is blind and deaf, instinct helps it find the pouch and it climbs in. There, the baby fastens its mouth to a nipple so it can feed on its mother's rich milk. The baby's mouth isn't developed enough to hang on, but the end of the nipple enlarges and fits into ridges in the tiny mouth so it can't let go.

This young koala must return regularly to its mother's pouch.

In the Pouch

The baby koala stays in its mother's pouch for about six months. During that time, its eyes open and it grows fur. Its back legs also develop, and during the last few weeks it spends in the pouch it kicks almost continually. Poor mom!

The little koala must learn to eat eucalyptus leaves. At first its mother feeds it pre-digested leaves. She provides this food from an opening just below her tail. That's why a downward-facing pocket is perfect for a koala. It makes it easy for the baby to reach its food supply.

Hang on tight!

Hello, World

When the baby first comes out of its mother's pouch, the world looks pretty frightening and it often climbs back in for shelter. That's tough on mom, especially when she's climbing. She must keep her stomach clear of any stubs on the tree that might hurt the baby in her pouch. However, things get easier once the baby moves onto its mom's back and rides around clasping her tightly with its arms. Being on the mother's back is also more comfortable for the baby. Why? When mom leaps from tree to tree she lands stomach first with quite a thud!

At first the baby is too scared to let go of its mom's fur to grab and eat leaves. But soon the smell of the eucalyptus becomes irresistible and the baby begins to feed.

After about five months the mother koala begins weaning her baby off milk.

Growing Up

A koala baby stays close to its mother for a few months after leaving her pouch. Even when it gets older, it will crawl onto her back if it is lonely or tired. Soon, however, mom refuses to let it climb on board and she lets the baby know that it is time for it to start a life of its own. If the baby is male, this means it may soon have to find its own territory.

As more and more trees in Australia are cut down to make room for houses and farms, it is becoming difficult for koalas to find places to live and feed. Many people are now working hard to help preserve this lovable animal's favorite eucalyptus trees. Thanks to their efforts, koalas will be able to continue to lead their sleepy lives high in Australia's treetops.

Koalas are strict but devoted mothers.

Words to Know

Camouflage   Fur or feathers that are colored so that they blend into the surroundings, making the animal difficult to see.

Cub   A young koala.

Den   An animal home.

Eucalyptus   Tall, broadleaf evergreen tree native to Australia.

Marsupial   An animal, such as the koala, that spends the first part of its life in a pouch in its mother's body.

Mate   To come together to produce young. Either member of an animal pair is also the other's mate.

Mating season   The time of the year when animals mate.

Nocturnal   Most active at night.

Territory   An area that an animal or group of animals lives in and usually defends from other animals of the same kind.

INDEX

Cover Photo: E.R. Degginger

Photo Credits: Bill Ivy, pages 4, 8, 12, 20, 27, 30, 35, 36, 46; Four By Five Inc., pages 7, 16; John Cancalosi, pages 11, 39, 40, 43; E.R. Degginger, page 15; Erwin and Peggy Bauer, pages 19, 23; Cincinnati Zoo, page 24; Australian Picture Library (The Stock Market Inc.), page 28; Kjell B. Sandved, pages 32, 44.